Australian
Show Cakes

Outstanding designs from the major cake decorating exhibitions

C&A CHILD & ASSOCIATES

AN ALL-AUSTRALIAN PUBLISHER

Published by
Child & Associates Publishing Pty Ltd,
9 Clearview Place, Brookvale, NSW, Australia, 2100
A wholly owned Australian publishing company
This book has been edited, designed and typeset
in Australia by the Publisher
Co-published in the U.K. and North America by Merehurst
Press, 5 Great James Street, London, WC1N 3DA
First Edition 1987

© Child & Associates Publishing Pty Ltd 1987

Text by Anne Thorpe
Photography by Gerard Young and Lennart Osbeck

Printed in Singapore by Colourwork Press Pte Ltd

**National Library of Australia Cataloguing-in-
Publication**

Australian Show Cakes.

 ISBN 0 86777 187 9.

 I. Cake decorating.

641.8'653

Back cover: A superb royal icing creation especially suited to a major show. The
showbag was made from royal icing then· flooded and hand-painted. The tiny clown
and farm animals were hand-moulded.

SHIRLEY VASS, NUNAWADING, VICTORIA

Contents

Introduction

This beautiful book is a catalogue of the
most outstanding cakes and cake decorating
ideas from the leading exhibitions around
Australia.

Most are major prize-winners while the
others are just so innovative that they had
to be included.

They have been created by many different
decorators whose skills are shown to their
best advantage by the superb photography.

Our thanks go to these talented people
whose many years of learning and practice
have resulted in this definitive reference of
cake decorating.

MRS DOREEN BURLEY, BUNDOORA, VICTORIA

Magnificent three-tiered wedding cake covered in subtle cream fondant. Each tier is scalloped and features extension work caught in the corners with tiny sprays of roses, forget-me-nots, maidenhair fern and inserted ribbon loops. The pillars were hand-made and decorated with embroidery to match the sides of the cake. The top has a superb hand-made vase featuring a floral spray that matches the sprays on the bottom two tiers. Tiny lace butterflies finish the cake.

MRS FRANCES DABB, BORONIA, VICTORIA

Superb three-tier octagonal-shaped wedding cake. The sprays on each tier consist of Cecil Bruner roses, violets, jasmine and baby fuchsias with fine embroidery on each side. The tiers are finished at the base with three rows of Garrett frills in deepening shades of pink which are topped with lace pieces.

MRS ROBYN HAMILTON, FERNTREE GULLY, VICTORIA

A large oval three-tier wedding cake on flooded boards. The floral decorations are made up of formal roses in pink with a lemon tint, orange blossom and pink boronia. Spirals of lace have been added to the hand-made pillars to match the sides of the cake. Heart-shaped motifs enhance each tier which is surrounded with fine extension work.

MRS A. BRYANT, BRIAN HILL, VICTORIA

A formal three-tier octagonal wedding cake. Magnificent mauve orchids, spotted sun orchids, pale pink boronia, yellow native pea and native violets decorate each tier. The hand-moulded basket on top is repeated in the side embroidery together with lace work which stands out from the cake. The pillars were hand-made and embroidered.

MRS KERRIE WALSH, CAMDEN, NEW SOUTH WALES

A cascade of tuber roses, white roses and primula link each
tier in this magnificent wedding cake. Embroidery of
primula adorns the sides of each tier and silver and white
ribbons finish the bouquets.

RUBY CONNELLY, TOUKLEY, NEW SOUTH WALES

A very unusual shape for a very traditional three-tier wedding cake. Formal roses and buds, Solomon's-seal and forget-me-nots adorn each tier together with ribbon loops and leaves. The very fine embroidery features roses and forget-me-nots with fern leaves. The roses were coloured with food colouring diluted with spirits and then dusted with petal dust.

MARIA BALUCI, BORONIA, VICTORIA

This is a very unusual presentation of a two-tier wedding cake. Both cakes have been surrounded with a double Garrett frill finished with fine lace. The top of each tier is decorated with full bloom roses, buds and leaves with *Gypsophila*, blossom and hyacinth.

RITA NICHOLLS, KYOGLE, NEW SOUTH WALES

A two-tier wedding cake made with unusual offcut diamond cakes. Sprays of Eucharist lilies, crucifix orchids, white blossoms and piped maidenhair fern adorn each tier. The top tier is supported by small wine glasses filled with mauve liquid to match the ribbons and embroidery. The end of each tier features extension work and a fine lace edge.

MRS RUBY MULLEY, CAWDOR, NEW SOUTH WALES

A clever idea to support the top tier is a feature of this wedding cake. The columns have been disguised by moulding the bridal couple and two bridesmaids around them. Tiny flowergirls have been added to complete the bridal party. Open roses and baby's breath form the beautiful floral display. Extension and lace work finish the edge and between the two rows of fine ribbon are tiny piped birds.

MRS JOY EAGLES, CAMDEN, NEW SOUTH WALES

This magnificent wedding cake features azaleas, mini orchids, *Gypsophila* and crucifix orchids spilling over two beautiful bell-shaped cakes. Narrow white ribbon loops intertwine through the flowers. The embroidery consists of forget-me-nots and daisies and the two mice on the horseshoe were flooded. Fine extension work and lace surrounds each bell.

MRS MAUREEN BALL, NORTH ESSENDON, VICTORIA.

This spendid two-tiered scalloped wedding cake features a heart-shaped motif on the side of each tier. The cake was decorated with pink roses and lilac. The tiny frame on top was made of royal icing decorated with lily-of-the-valley to match the embroidery on the sides of the cake. The bride and groom were flooded on the plaque.

MRS CHERYL BLOOR, NORTH PARRAMATTA, NEW SOUTH WALES

A classically beautiful wedding cake with the serenity of two swans floating on top. The floral sprays are made up of pixie carnations, baby's breath, Solomon's-seal, ivy leaves and *Bouvardia*. The pink frosting under the extension work is enhanced by the pale pink tips on the lace work. The bottom tier has two pairs of doves and the two beautifully sculptured swans adorn the top.

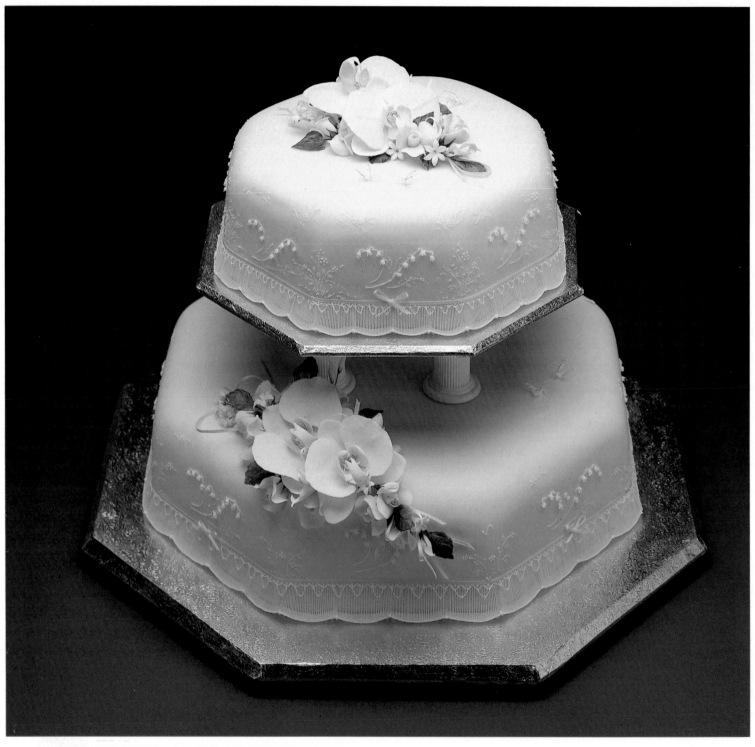

JUDY JOHNSTONE, WENTWORTHVILLE, NEW SOUTH WALES

Phalaenopsis orchids with Cecil Bruner roses and hyacinths are the central feature of this cake. The beautiful extension work features ribbon insertions and lily-of-the-valley embroidery.

GEMMA JOHANSSEN, HURSTVILLE, NEW SOUTH WALES

A striking colour scheme is the main feature of this cake. A perfectly plain white cake has been lifted with fine embroidery of black chantilly lace. Black and white orchids and white blossom form the centre spray. The tiny black spots on the extension work continue the theme of the board covering.

AUDREY KING, EAST DONCASTER, VICTORIA

A traditional birthday cake to delight any mum. This large oval is decorated with a spray of azaleas, quince blossom and maidenhair fern inserted with ribbon loops. The side of the cake features fine embroidery and lace work which stands out from the cake. The scalloped extension work around the base is a magnificent finishing touch.

LOUISE DAVY, LAVINGTON, NEW SOUTH WALES

A simple oval shape is the base for this masterpiece in painting. The traditional farm scene was painted in true earth colours and the scene around the side is continuous showing again the true artist at work. The base features a white beading surrounded by coloured piped loops which are curved.

MRS ROBYN NOLAN, HAWTHORN, VICTORIA

An old-fashioned touch to a pretty cake. After covering, the centre was cut out of this fondant and replaced with cream icing. The design was then flooded on and the girls added. Hand-moulded pink rosebuds and blossoms in white surround the plaque. The ribbons are caught in the lace. The lace is piped and flooded and is an original design.

LOUISE DAVY, LAVINGTON, NEW SOUTH WALES

Victoria Plum adorns this simple scalloped cake. The background was flooded in with water wash and the butterflies were flooded, then dried and hand-painted. The top was flooded in royal icing. There is brush embroidery on the sides and the base of the cake features piped plum blossom with tiny a moulded blossom in each scallop.

GEMMA JOHANSSEN, HURSTVILLE, NEW SOUTH WALES

A birthday cake decorated to enhance the lovely scalloped
shape. Frangipanis and yellow blossom were moulded and
hand-painted and arranged in simple sprays at each corner
of the board and a circular arrangement was placed on top.
Ribbons in colours to match the lettering and the extension
work curve around each scallop. The base of extension work
features forget-me-nots.

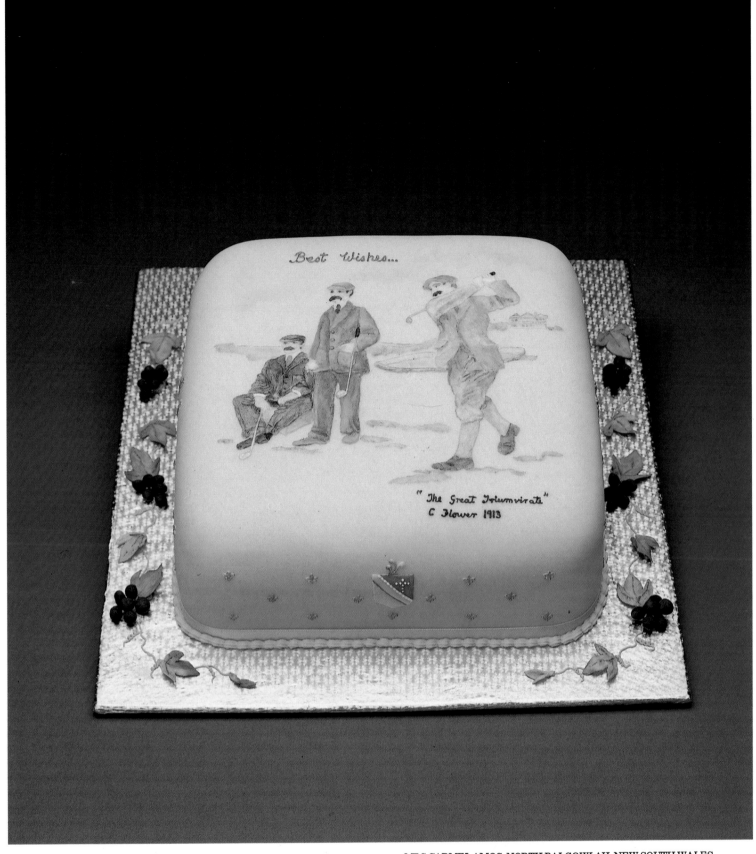

Best Wishes...

"The Great Triumvirate"
C Flower 1913

MRS CARMEL AMOS, NORTH BALGOWLAH, NEW SOUTH WALES

This unusual male birthday cake features a faithful
reproduction of a 1913 painting 'The Great Triumvirate' by
C. Flower. The figures were flooded on and moulded black
grapes and leaves were placed on the board. Fleurs-de-lis in
gold were added to the sides of the cake with a shield placed
on the front and back. The sky was shaded with petal dust .

MRS DOROTHY SILVA, ST ARNAUD, VICTORIA

A charming birthday design, this oval cake was covered in
coffee-coloured icing. The side decorations feature pink
blossom trailing up over the sides to the top. The lady was
flooded on and her feather boa was piped.

LORRAINE SIMPSON, BALWYN, VICTORIA

A very different idea for dad's birthday. The beer stein was made from a loaf-tin shaped cake. It was covered in almond icing and then rolled fondant. The design was traced on and then hand-painted and the ashtray was shaped with almond paste and covered in rolled fondant. The ivy, pipe, handle and lid were all moulded from fondant and hand-painted.

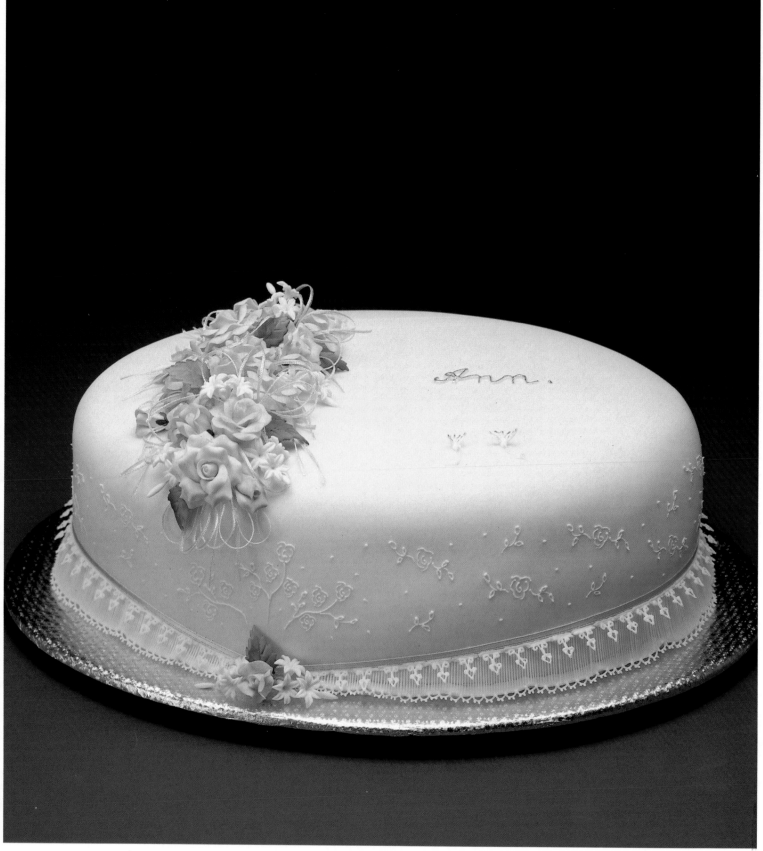

MRS ROYSLIN E. KITCHING, SOUTH WENTWORTHVILLE, NEW SOUTH WALES

An elegant birthday cake with a traditional spray of Dorothy Perkins roses intertwined with fine pink ribbons. The extension and lace work falls to a single point at the front and is finished off with a small rose and blossom.

SUE O'LOUGHLIN, EAST KEYLORE, VICTORIA

An elaborate cake for a special christening. The centre plaque was done with floodwork and inset into the cake with a picture frame. Cecil Bruner roses and *Gypsophila* with lemon and white ribbon loops surround the paschal candle and scroll. A Garrett frill surrounds the base giving an eyelet effect to simulate broderie anglaise. The lace on the christening robe is double the edge lace.

MRS NOELLE BARNARD, CARNEGIE, VICTORIA

A fairytale christening cake to 'Welcome Baby'. The design is done with floodwork which has been lifted and piped. Each end has been enhanced with extension work and the lace work is a combination of lace and flooding. The final touch is the scalloped board which frames the cake. The lettering was flooded then lifted off.

MRS V. SEIDEL-DAVIES, WEST FOOTSCRAY, VICTORIA

A christening cake with a delicate touch. The delightful possum design was flooded on with hand-moulded apple blossom on the base. The lace work also continues the apple blossom theme.

MARYANNE MONTEBELLO, AUBURN, NEW SOUTH WALES

A sleeping baby is the theme for this christening cake. A church window was painted on top and the yellow bows were flooded on. The doves on the sides add to the theme of peace and serenity. The sprays consist of dainty lemon and white flowers.

LOUISE DAVY, LAVINGTON, NEW SOUTH WALES

This very unusual design for a christening cake was flat washed (not chalked) with floodwork on top. The tiny bees around the base were flooded then dried, hand-painted and placed on the cake. The base is finished off with lace in a five-petal flower.

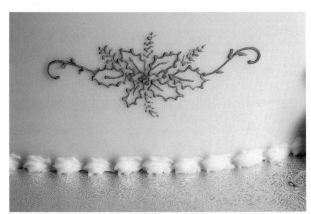

MRS J. O'NEILL, FOREST HILL, VICTORIA

The real spirit of Christmas is shown in this cake which features a flood-work motif with some modelling. The royal icing collar was made separately then placed in position. Modelling paste was used to form the clown and other motifs around the base. The delicate holly embroidery is the finishing touch.

MRS SANDRA JONES, WANTIRNA, VICTORIA

A cake with the real spirit of Christmas. The top spray consists of fuchsias, holly leaves, red berries, pine needles and the centres of immature pine cones. All these were exquisitely hand-painted and arranged with loops of red and white ribbon. The base features double extension work and the leaves on the sides were moulded and hand-painted. Holly leaves and berries form the lace work.

LOUISE DAVY, LAVINGTON, NEW SOUTH WALES

A very Australian Christmas cake. The background was water washed and the top and sides flooded. The grass was painted with food colouring and the scene around the sides is continuous. The unusual red and green geometric lace and the red foil enhance the whole mood of an Australian Christmas.

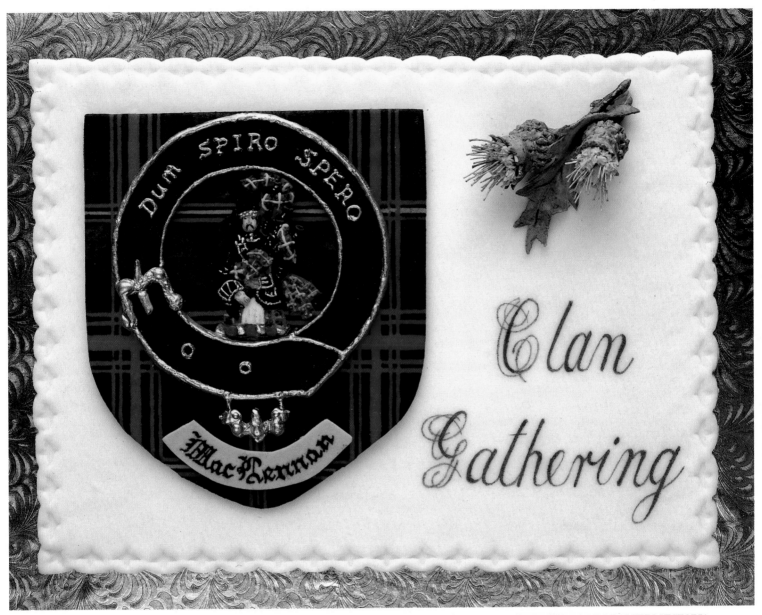

LORRAINE SIMPSON, BALWYN, VICTORIA

This Scottish plaque was made from rolled fondant and the shield, also made from rolled fondant, was added later. The MacLennan tartan was drawn on in pencil and then painted with many coats to attain the depth of colour. The piper was moulded and placed on later with the scroll and the thistle. The lettering was hand-painted.

LOUISE DAVY, LAVINGTON, NEW SOUTH WALES

Hand-moulded open roses with occasional buds lie on the
frame of this serene painting. The base consists of two
layers of fondant with the centre cut from the top layer. The
scene was flooded.

MRS BERYL BARCLAY, NUNAWADING, VICTORIA

This is an ideal plaque for a young girl. The forget-me-nots, roses, tulips and wisteria were hand-moulded and the umbrella was made by piping on tulle. The figures were flooded with royal icing with the arm of each being placed on later. The wheel and birds were also flooded. The fine lace work that surrounds the plaque is done in the shape of flower petals.

41

MISS LISA J. BARNARD, CARNEGIE, VICTORIA

A fun idea for any cake. This charming design was triple flooded in royal icing with the small items being made from fondant and hand-painted. The hippo was made from royal icing then hand-painted.

J. DINGEMANS, LAVERTON, VICTORIA

A birthday card made of royal icing is the base for this design. The royal icing was hardened using gum tragacanth. The roses and carnations were made from modelling paste and the whole design mounted on black velvet.

43

MRS ROBYN HAMILTON, FERNTREE GULLY, VICTORIA

This bridal display arranged on a bible features double and
single fuchsias with violets and lily-of-the-valley. The
design is surrounded by lace and embroidery and is
mounted on green corduroy.

MRS A. BRYANT, BRIAR HILL, VICTORIA

This elegant arrangement of hand-moulded flowers
consists of cattalier orchids, Cecil Bruner roses, jasmine
and *Gypsophila*. The spray is edged with lace and ribbon,
and is mounted on a dome of white satin.

MRS RUBY MULLEY, CAWDOR, NEW SOUTH WALES

The base of this royal icing fan features a spray of roses, fuchsias, *Gypsophila* and *Eriostemon*. Narrow white ribbon loops peep through the flowers and wide pink ribbons complete the bow.

"Schlumbergera"
Zygo Cactus
(Pink)

JOY EAGLES, CAMDEN, NEW SOUTH WALES

A fun design for the novelty section this true-to-life cactus
was hand-moulded and then painted. Coloured royal icing
crumbled to resemble the dirt is the finishing touch. The
pot was shaped in rolled fondant around the cake.

MRS NOLA CORDELL, LAVERTON, VICTORIA

A masterpiece of design to delight children and adults alike. The base board was covered in green suede contact and the bed made from a 25 cm (10 in) square cake cut into an oblong and raised on a slightly larger separate board. The pillow was made from fondant as were the hands and feet of the sick rabbit. A lump of icing was used for the body. The bed linen was crafted in rolled fondant and the brown blanket was given the nap effect by hitting it gently with a brush. The quilt was made from icing that was hand-worked with colour to give a slightly streaky effect. It was then rolled and cut and stuck to the blanket with egg white. The bed ends were made from modelling paste.

The doctor was made from a cone-shaped piece of fruit cake, covered with almond paste and dressed with rolled fondant. The head was made from modelling paste, stuck with royal icing and supported with a skewer. Stamens were used for whiskers and eyelashes and the glasses were made from modelling paste and then painted. The log was made from a slice of log fruit cake covered with rolled fondant. Modelling paste was used to make the pebbles and flowers.

MRS A. A. McMASTER, YARRAVILLE, VICTORIA

A true Australian-designed cake. A digger's hat shaped with almond paste then completely covered again with more almond paste. The fondant was specially coloured and the crown was covered first. The brim of 8 cm (20 in) was then added together with a hand-made band. The badges and medals were made of modelling paste and hand-painted.

RITA NICHOLLS, KYOGLE, NEW SOUTH WALES

This Australian Akubra, made from cake covered with almond paste and rolled fondant, makes a marvellous twenty-first birthday cake. A small spray of flannel flowers, bottlebrush, wattle and gumnuts continues the Australian bush theme. The leather-look band and free-standing saddle are embossed.

51

CAROLINE LACK, SOUTH YARRA, VICTORIA

A most unusual subject for a cake, this punk was made by shaping the cake with almond icing then covering it in modelling paste. The body was made first then the legs were added. The limbs were attached with wooden skewers then the body was dressed with modelling paste clothes. The head was added last and a garlic press was used for the hair. The whole thing was then hand-painted.

TERRY ROSS, BAIRNSDALE, VICTORIA

True Italian spirit is shown in this modelling paste sculpture. The bottle was made by covering the cake in rolled fondant and then using modelling paste to make the basket. All the other items were hand-moulded with modelling paste then hand-painted with food colouring.

EVAN JONES, ZETLAND, NEW SOUTH WALES

A fantasy of design this magnificent beehive has taken great patience to create. A multi-tiered cake was covered in fondant, then hand-coloured to achieve the mottled effect. The bees, toadstools, pebbles, snail and ladybird were moulded from fondant icing then hand-painted. The flowers were wired in sprays and then positioned. The blackberries were piped from royal icing and wired into the cake. The bees were fitted with black tulle wings and wired into position.

MRS DOROTHY SILVA, ST ARNAUD, VICTORIA

A superbly made cake in a most unusual design. The bull was made from two log cakes attached with wooden skewers. The cakes were covered with almond paste and moulded into shape. The whole thing was covered with royal icing which was specially coloured (not painted). The icing was flicked to give the hide effect. The eyes were moulded then painted and placed in position. The lashes were piped.

MRS NANCY GRIFFITHS, LOWER TEMPLESTOWE, VICTORIA

A hen and her chicks realistically shown on the farm. The hen was made by covering the cake with rolled fondant. The head and tail were formed from crescent shapes. The top of the wing was flooded then hand-painted and the feathers were moulded and painted individually. The chickens were made using stipple work and were flooded. The eggs were moulded around real eggs and the gravel was made from modelling paste put through a blender.

MRS LYNETTE THOMPSON, LOWER TEMPLESTOWE, VICTORIA

58

Beautifully designed ballet shoes and case in the palest pink. The ballerina was flooded on the case and rolled fondant was used for the handle and latch. The shoes were shaped with modelling paste then covered with rolled fondant to attain smoothness. The whole design is enhanced with wide satin ribbons in matching pale pink.

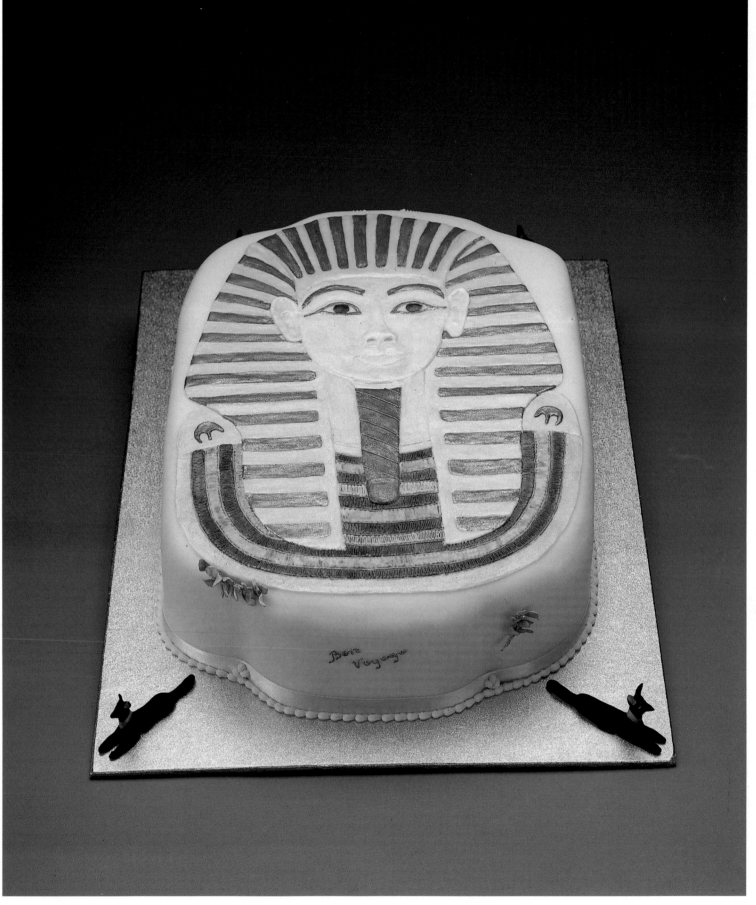

MRS CARMEL AMOS, NORTH BALGOWLAH, NEW SOUTH WALES

Bon Voyage to Egypt is the theme here with a superb mask of Tutankhamun in three-dimensional design. Hand-painted in non-toxic metallic finish it is a fine adornment to an otherwise simple cake.

MRS JOY EAGLES, CAMDEN, NEW SOUTH WALES

This large chocolate egg made from dark and white
chocolate is decorated with fine lace work. The flowers are
double and single azaleas, violets and hyacinths with pale
pink ribbons. The rabbit was flooded.

MRS R. HURTADO, SYLVANIA, NEW SOUTH WALES

A rich chocolate egg is colourfully adorned here with bright
orange and yellow poppies, daisies and ivy leaves. The
narrow ribbons intertwine among the flowers and the
embroidery features forget-me-nots.